Oxford First Encyclopedia

People
and
Places

Andrew Langley

OXFORD

OXFORD
UNIVERSITY PRESS

Great Clarendon Street, Oxford OX2 6DP

Oxford University Press is a department of the University of Oxford.
It furthers the University's objective of excellence in research, scholarship,
and education by publishing worldwide in

Oxford New York

Auckland Bangkok Buenos Aires Cape Town Chennai
Dar es Salaam Delhi Hong Kong Istanbul Karachi Kolkata
Kuala Lumpur Madrid Melbourne Mexico City Mumbai Nairobi
São Paulo Shanghai Taipei Tokyo Toronto

Oxford is a registered trade mark of Oxford University Press
in the UK and in certain other countries

© Andrew Langley 1999, 2002

The moral rights of the author have been asserted

Database right Oxford University Press (maker)

First published in 1999
Second edition 2002

British Library Cataloguing in Publication Data available

ISBN 0-19-910972-9

10 9 8 7 6 5 4 3

Printed in Malaysia

Contents

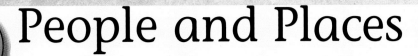

People and Places

You live on the Earth, together with millions of other people. Some people live in villages, some in crowded cities, some on wide plains, some in forests and some in the mountains. But all of us need the same basic things – food, shelter, a family and friends. We find these things in many different ways.

Families

Do you live on your own? Or are you part of a family? A family is a group of people who are related to each other. They care for each other, and share money, food and housework. You are most closely related to your parents, brothers and sisters. But you have many other relatives.

My great-grandparents' generation

great-grandfather   great-grandmother   great-grandfather   great-grandmother   great-grandfather   great-grandmother   great-grandfather   great-grandmother

My grandparents' generation

great uncle   great aunt   grandfather   grandmother   grandfather   grandmother   great uncle   great aunt

My parents' generation

uncle   aunt   father   mother   uncle   aunt

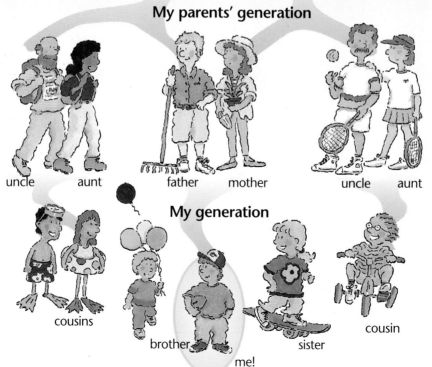

My generation

cousins   brother   me!   sister   cousin

This is called a family "tree". Actually, it looks more like a net or a web. It shows how members of a family are related to each other. The tree is divided into different "generations". In each generation, the people are about the same age.

6

Different families

You may live in a small family – just you and one or two parents, perhaps brothers and sisters too. But not all family groups are the same. In some families only one parent lives with the children. Other families are much bigger, with children, parents, grandparents, aunts, uncles and cousins all living together in an extended family.

Babies every second!

There are more than 5,800 million people in the world. And every day about 400,000 more babies are born. That's 255 every minute!

◁ Many families live together in this big house in Borneo. Up to fifty families may have their home in one "longhouse".

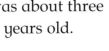

Family likeness

People often look similar to their brothers or sisters, or to their mother or father. We inherit the way we look from our parents. Can you guess the connection between these three children? They are a girl, her mother, and her grandmother. Each of them was photographed when she was about three years old.

Find out about your family

Find out about your own family tree. Ask older people in your family to help you. See how far back in time you can go. Where do your grandparents come from? What about your great-grandparents? When were they born? What jobs did they do?

Where we live

We all have a place to live in, which we call home. Your home has a roof and walls to protect you from the weather. It is the place where you eat and go to sleep, where you and your family can be together.

Our homes come in all shapes and sizes, from tall apartment buildings in cities to small shelters made by people in hot countries to shade them from the sun. Houses such as caravans and tents can even move from place to place.

What are houses made of?

People build their houses out of many different materials. Some houses are built with materials that can easily be found nearby, such as wood, stone or clay. Other houses may be built from materials such as concrete, steel and glass, which may be made in faraway factories.

△ A giant block of flats in Bombay, India, built of modern materials. The frame inside is made of steel girders, the walls and floors are concrete. There are lots of large glass windows.

△ This house in southern Africa is made of clay. Clay is good for building houses – as long as there isn't too much rain! In wetter countries, the clay is baked into bricks to make it waterproof.

△ A stone house in Edinburgh, Scotland. This house was built from blocks of stone cut out of the local rocks. The roof is made of slate, another kind of stone.

8

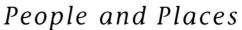 In big cities like Tokyo in Japan, thousands of people live and work close together. Cities are busy and noisy, but they have plenty of shops, hospitals, buses and other useful services.

Villages, towns and cities

Our homes are usually grouped together. A few people, like farmers, live in houses which are built on their own, in the middle of large areas of land. A village is a small group of homes in a rural area. Some villages grow into towns, and some towns into big cities. Where would you rather live – in a city, a town, or in the countryside?

Underground cities

In crowded cities, people build skyscrapers upwards. But in Japan, builders are now thinking of going downwards. They are planning cities under the ground, where over 100,000 people will live and work. Sunlight for these underground cities will be reflected down from the surface by mirrors!

△ This Mongolian tent is called a yurt. The family need a home that is easy to move, because they travel from place to place with their herds of animals. The covering is of thick felt, fitted over a wooden frame.

△ This log house in Russia is made of wood, cut from the forests all around. There is plenty of firewood to keep the house warm through the long, cold winters.

Life in a town

A town is like a huge, complicated machine. It has thousands of different parts, which all have to work together to make it run smoothly. There are the buildings – shops, offices, houses and factories. Between the buildings are roads for cars, lorries, bicycles and buses. But the most important parts of all are the people who live and work in the town.

Keeping a town running

A town needs more than just roads and buildings to keep it going. Food has to be brought in by truck or train, and water comes in pipes from big lakes called reservoirs. People need buses and trains to get around. The town needs rubbish collectors, and sewage pipes to get rid of dirty water. It also needs people to keep everything running.

What can you find?

Look at this busy town. It has grown from a small old town to a large new one. See if you can spot all the things in the list below. Some of them are easy to find – others are harder!

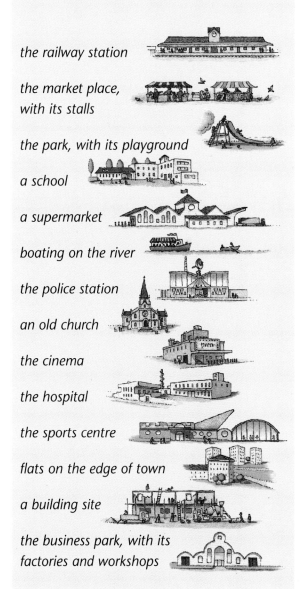

the railway station

the market place, with its stalls

the park, with its playground

a school

a supermarket

boating on the river

the police station

an old church

the cinema

the hospital

the sports centre

flats on the edge of town

a building site

the business park, with its factories and workshops

People at work

Most of us have to work. You work at school. Grown-ups work at thousands of different kinds of jobs. They do this so that they can provide food and clothes for their families and look after them. Some people grow their own food or make their clothes. Others are paid money for their work. With this money they can buy food, clothes and other things they need.

▽ The Masai people of East Africa are very proud of their cattle. They rarely eat them for meat. Instead they drink the animals' milk and blood.

▽ These fishermen from Japan catch fish in huge nets. Their boat is called a trawler.

Hunters and gatherers

The simplest way to get food is to catch it yourself. For thousands of years, people have gathered fruit and vegetables, and hunted animals. If they do not find anything, they go hungry! Today, there are still hunters and gatherers in a few parts of the world. And there are many other people, like fishermen, who catch food to sell.

Growers and herders

Farmers and herders use the land to grow food. Farmers plough the land and sow crops, such as wheat and rice. Or they look after animals – cattle, pigs, sheep, goats and chickens. Herders travel with their animals. If there is not enough grass for the herd, they move on. From the animals they get meat and other things they need, such as milk and wool.

Makers

Some people work at making things for others to buy. Craft workers use their hands and simple tools to make beautiful objects such as clay pots or woollen rugs. In factories, people use machines to make all sorts of goods, from cars to toothbrushes.

People who help us

Many workers do not make or grow anything. They may work in offices, banks or libraries. They may sell things in shops. Or they may help other people. Nurses and doctors look after us when we are sick. Bus and train drivers take us from place to place. Police officers and firefighters help to protect us and our property.

△ To make patterned rugs, these Indian women must first spin the wool on a spinning wheel, then dye it different colours. They then weave the different colours together on a loom.

△ Firefighters wear special protective clothes for fighting fires. They carry air tanks and breathing masks, so that they do not choke on the smoke inside burning buildings.

13

People at play

School's over! Work's finished! What are you going to do in your free time? Two hundred years ago, people had little time for fun. They worked long hours, and only had one day off a week. This still happens in many parts of the world today. But now machines do a lot of our work for us. We have more free time than before – and many more ways of enjoying it.

Relaxing

Many people like to relax in their free time. They might take it easy at home, chatting with friends or reading. They might also go out, to the park or to the cinema. But the most popular way of relaxing is to watch television.

△ Parks are good places to relax. People go there to play in the playground, have a picnic, play games – or just to go for a stroll.

Playing sport

There are hundreds of different sports and games to choose from. Some can be played almost anywhere. You can play football in the park, or in your garden. You can play baseball on a beach. But other sports, like skiing or swimming, need special settings or equipment.

Playground games

Children have always made up their own games to play. Some, like hide-and-seek, are played all over the world. But others are less well-known. Here are two for you to try.

Ear and nose (from Iran)
Stand in a circle. One person pulls the ear, or nose, or hair of the person to the left (gently!). They do the same to the person on their left – and so on, round the circle. Then the first player starts again, and pulls a different part of the body. You must not laugh. If you do, you are out.

"Keep the cattle in" (from Botswana)
All the players except two hold hands in a ring and move slowly round. The two players inside the ring are the "cattle". As the ring moves round, the cattle try to run out under people's arms. If they get out, they join the ring, and the ones who let them escape become the cattle.

◁ Football is a very old game. A kind of football was probably played in China over 2,000 years ago. Soccer is the most popular football game in the world.

△ Basketball is a game for two teams of players. To score points you have to throw the ball into your opponent's basketball net.

Going on holiday

Every year, millions of people go away on holiday. They may go to the seaside or countryside in their own country, or they may go abroad. Modern aircraft can take us far from home very quickly. It is possible to fly 5,500 kilometres from New York to Paris in about seven hours!

What we eat

We all have to eat to stay alive. Good food gives us energy and keeps our bodies healthy. It is also fun to cook and eat. Around the world, people have learned to prepare the food they grow or buy in many different ways. But in all parts of the world, a healthy meal has the same types of food in it.

A healthy meal

The biggest part of a healthy meal is something filling, like rice, bread or potatoes. This is called a "staple" food. With this staple food we eat vegetables or fruit, and a food with plenty of protein, such as meat, fish or beans. "Dairy products" – things like milk and cheese – are also good protein foods.

◁ This picture shows some of the foods we need for a healthy diet. Can you work out which are staple foods?

Favourite foods in . . .

People in different parts of the world eat very different meals! Here are some examples from around the world.

Italy

Pizza. The base is made from bread dough. This is covered with cheese, tomatoes and many other toppings. The bread dough is made from wheat.

The USA

Beefburgers, chips and beans. The beef comes from cattle. The potatoes for the chips come from plants grown in the fields. The beans are from plants, too.

Africa

Groundnut stew with fufu. The stew is chicken cooked in a groundnut (peanut) sauce. Fufu are dumplings made from vegetables such as cassava, yams or potatoes.

Japan

Japanese people eat a lot of fish, and it is often served raw. Sashimi is raw fish, radish and seaweed, served with soy sauce and raw vegetables carved in the shapes of flowers.

Faraway foods

Some of the food you buy may have travelled a long way to get to the shops. Here's how to find out where your food has come from. Go to your store cupboard or fridge, and look at the tins and packets inside. Read the labels carefully. Somewhere it will tell you where the food was grown or packed. For instance, a pack of butter may say "Produce of New Zealand". A tin of tomatoes may say "Produce of Italy". If there's a country you do not know, look it up on a world map.

What we believe

Most people have a religion. This means that they believe in a power outside their ordinary lives. They often have a name for this power – a God or gods. There are hundreds of different religions in the world. Each religion has its own way of worshipping its God or gods, and a special set of rules for its believers.

▷ Hannukah is the Jewish festival of lights. To celebrate, people light candles on a special Hannukah candlestick.

Judaism

Judaism is the religion of the Jews. Like the Christians and Muslims, they believe that there is one God, who made the world. The homeland of the Jews is Israel in the Middle East, but Jews now live in many parts of the world. Saturday is the Jewish day of prayer, when Jews rest from work. They go to a service in a synagogue, their place of worship. They read from the Torah and the Book of Prophets, their holy books.

Christianity

Christians follow the teachings of Jesus Christ. They believe he was God's son who came to live on Earth, where he was put to death on a cross, and then came to life again. There are many different Christian groups. One of the biggest is the Roman Catholic Church. Sunday is the holy day for Christians. They go to a church to worship God and Jesus Christ.

▷ Christians celebrate the birth of Jesus at Christmas by singing carols.

People and Places

Islam

People who follow the Islamic religion are Muslims. They believe that there is one God, called Allah. They follow the teachings of the Prophet Mohammed, who lived in Arabia long ago. Muslims must follow five strict rules. They must believe in Allah, pray five times each day, give money to the poor, travel at least once to the holy city of Mecca, and fast (eat no daytime food) for one month each year.

▽ Ramadan is the Muslim special month of fasting. At the end of the month, they celebrate!

Hinduism

Hindus give God many names. Among the most important are Brahma, who made the world, Vishnu, who preserves life, and Shiva, who destroys life. Hindus believe that, after we die, we are born again in a new form. Hinduism is the main religion of India and Nepal, and is important in countries such as Sri Lanka and Indonesia. Many Hindus have special places in their homes called shrines, decorated with statues or pictures of their favourite gods.

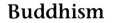

△ Diwali is the Hindu festival of lights, at their New Year. Children make special patterns with coloured sand, called Rangoli patterns.

▽ Wesak is the most important Buddhist festival. People decorate their houses and the streets with lanterns and candles.

Buddhism

Buddhists have no gods. They believe that unhappiness and pain are caused by human greed. Buddhists find happiness by living a simple life. They follow the teachings of an Indian prince, who became known as the Buddha. Each day, they spend time meditating. They sit still and quiet and relax their minds, to forget the selfishness of everyday life.

19

Children of the world

What would it be like to live in another country? Many parts of your life would be very different – your home, your school, your games, your holidays. Here are children from around the world to tell you about their lives.

My name is Natasha. I live in a city in Russia. My home is a tiny flat. We have to share the kitchen and bathroom with our neighbours. Winters are very cold, and I wear a fur hat and coat to school. On summer weekends we all go to our other home in the countryside. There, we can climb trees and hunt for mushrooms.

My name is Moktar. I live in the desert in Mali. My family does not stay in one place. We have to get food for our goats and camels – and food is hard to find here. So we are often on the move. My home is a tent, and I wear a white cloth round my head to protect me from the burning sun.

My name is Kathleen. I live in a village in Ireland. The nearest town is over 15 kilometres away. We have a small house with a big garden, where we keep two goats and some hens. In summer, I like to play outside with my pet kitten Jess. But in winter, I sit in front of a cosy fire and watch television.

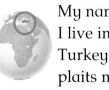

My name is Fatima. I live in a city in Turkey. My mother plaits my long hair every morning, ready for school. Lessons finish at lunchtime. In the afternoon, my mother sends me to buy fruit and vegetables at the market. I take care to choose only the best and cheapest. As a reward, I buy a snack of baked lamb wrapped in bread.

People and Places

  My name is Mariam. I live in a village in Tanzania. Before I go to school, I have work to do. I fetch water from the well, then drive my family's nine cows out into the fields. But when school is over, there is plenty of time for fun. I play football, or make wooden toys for my little brothers and sisters.

My name is Greg. I live outside a small town in the USA. My brother and I have a long walk to catch the bus that takes us to school in the town. In winter, when it snows, the walk takes even longer. That is because we have snowball fights! In summer, Mum and Dad take us camping in the mountains.

My name is Sanjay. I live in a village in India. My family is poor, so my brothers all go out to work. But I am lucky – I go to school. I get up early each morning and walk to the school. When it gets very hot, we have lessons outside in the shade of a tree.

My name is Inga. I live in a small town in Sweden. The land is very flat here, so I like to go out on my bicycle. When it is snowy, I ski to school. We start lessons very early – at 8 o'clock! Once a week I have dancing lessons. I am also learning to play the violin.

21

Music and dance

Music is a set of sounds – but not just any sounds. They need to please or excite us. The sounds are usually arranged to make a tune. Different sounds can also be played together to make harmonies. Music needs a regular beat, or rhythm, and rhythm is a vital part of dancing. This is why music and dance so often go together.

Making music

You can make music in all sorts of ways. You can sing with your voice, either on your own, or with other people. You can hit an instrument, such as a drum or a gong. You can blow into an instrument such as a saxophone or a whistle. You can pluck the strings of an instrument such as a guitar. Each part of the world has its own kind of music, and its own instruments to play it on.

Dancing about

Do you jump up and down when you are excited? That is a kind of dancing! In most dances, people move their bodies in time to music or a rhythm. At parties and special celebrations, people dance together to enjoy themselves. But there are other kinds of dancing, which are performed for people to watch. The dancers often wear costumes, and train for many years to learn the skills they need.

Make your own music

You can have your very own orchestra with these simple instruments.

Scratcher: *wrap sandpaper round two small blocks of wood. Then rub the blocks together in a regular rhythm.*

Kazoo: *wrap a piece of greaseproof paper round a comb. Press the comb against your mouth and hum.*

Musical straws: *flatten one end of a straw, and snip it to a point. Blow hard down the straw to make a sound. Straws of different lengths will make different notes.*

Painting and sculpture

We like to make pictures. Some show what
we see around us. Others are pictures of
imaginary things. Over thousands of years,
we have learned many ways of making
these pictures. We can put paint marks
on paper, or canvas – or even walls.
We can carve figures out of wood or stone.
We can make shapes with metal or clay.

△ Many Christian churches have
windows made of stained, or
coloured, glass. The pictures on
them often tell stories from the Bible.

What are pictures for?

Paintings and sculptures can have lots of uses. They can tell stories, about anything from great adventures to everyday events. They can show gods or saints and can be used as holy objects. They can show what famous people looked like.
But, most of all, pictures are something to enjoy!

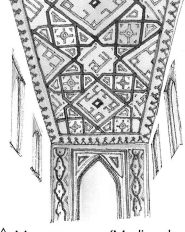

▷ This gold mask shows the face of a king who died in Greece over 3,500 years ago.

△ Many mosques (Muslim places of prayer) have tiled patterns all over the walls and ceilings. The patterns are beautiful combinations of shapes and colours.

△ This picture is a copy of a painting by an Italian artist. It shows a scene from the story of Saint George and the dragon. Saint George was a knight who fought and killed a fierce dragon to stop it from eating the king's daughter.

△ The children in this picture are using all kinds of materials to make pictures and models. How many different kinds of material can you see?

◁ These hand prints were done for fun. The bright colours and bold shapes look happy and full of energy.

Telling stories

Everybody likes a story. Even before people had learned to write, they told stories to each other out loud. Today, we have many ways of telling stories. In a play or a film, the actors use movement and speech. They pretend to be the people in the tale. In a book, the author uses written words to tell us what happens.

Acting out stories

People first performed plays in Greece, over 2,500 years ago. A Greek theatre had no roof, and the audience sat on stone seats. Since then, many different kinds of plays (or drama) have grown up, in different parts of the world.

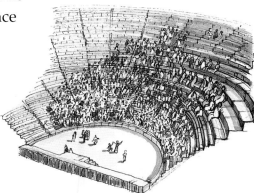

Stories in books

The easiest place to find a good story is in your local library. Most towns have their own library, packed with thousands of books. Some stories will be very old, and were first written down many centuries ago. Others will be brand new, for new stories are being written all the time.

▽ In this shadow play, there are puppets instead of actors. A light behind the flat puppets throws their shadows on to a screen.

△ A theatre in ancient Greece. The ruins of many old theatres can still be seen today.

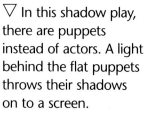

△ A modern theatre with a raised stage, powerful lights and realistic scenery.

People and Places

Stories on film

On a film, you can see the actors. What you cannot see are the dozens of other people who help to make the film. Some people film the action with the camera, or record the words and sounds. Some people work the powerful lights which make each scene look clear. Some people make the scenery, or special effects such as rain or snow. Most important of all is the director, who is in charge of everyone else.

Make a flip book

You can make your own moving pictures! Take a sheet of A4 paper, and ask an adult to help you cut it into 16 equal pieces. Draw a picture of a figure on the first piece. Now carefully copy that figure on to the second piece, but with a small difference: perhaps the arms have moved a little. Draw a figure on each of the other pieces, each time changing it a little. Now staple your pieces together in order, and try quickly flipping through the pages. Your figure will seem to move!

◁ Action films often have scenes where the actors have to do difficult and dangerous tricks. These scenes are often done by special actors called "stunt people". In this picture, the stunt man is dropping from an aeroplane on to a moving truck.

27

Glossary

business park a place in a town or city where there are a lot of offices and small factories.

cassava a plant grown in hot countries. It has roots that can be eaten, like the roots of potatoes or carrots.

cattle cows and bulls.

city a place where a lot of people live. A city is bigger than a town.

concrete a mixture of water, sand, cement and gravel, which sets hard to make a strong material for building.

crops plants that farmers grow for food, like wheat or rice.

dairy products milk, and foods that are made from milk. Cheese, butter and yoghurt are dairy products.

desert an area where hardly any rain falls. Few plants and animals can live there because it is so dry.

dough a thick mixture of flour and water, used for making things like bread and rolls.

drama writing or acting in plays.

factory a large building where machines are used to make things.

fasting not eating food, usually for religious reasons.

fibres thin strands or threads. Wool and cotton are made up of fibres.

girder a long beam, usually made of steel. Girders are joined together to make the frameworks of buildings and bridges.

harmony musical notes that sound good when they are sung or played together.

relative a member of your family, such as your father or grandfather, sister, aunt or cousin.

reservoir a lake where water is stored for drinking or for making electricity. Often it is made by damming a river.

rhythm the regular pattern of beats or sounds in a piece of music.

shrine a place devoted to a holy person or object.

skyscraper a building so tall that it seems to "scrape the sky".

staple food the most important food grown or eaten in a region.

Torah the holy book of Jewish people.

town a place where lots of people live together. A town is smaller than a city.

trawler a kind of fishing boat that catches fish in a large net pulled behind it.

yam a kind of vegetable eaten in hot countries.

yurt a kind of tent that has a light wooden frame with a thick felt covering. It is also called a "ger".

Index

Index

Acknowledgements

Abbreviations: t = top; b = bottom; c = centre; l = left; r = right; (back) = background; (fore) = foreground.

Illustrations

Cover George Smith; cover tr Ellen Beier; back cover t Julian Baum; back cover b Patricia Ludlow; 3 Ellen Beier; 4 Scot Ritchie; 5 Georgie Birkett; 6 Scot Ritchie; 7br Scot Ritchie; 8bl, bc, br, 9bl, bc Julian Baker; 9cr Scot Ritchie 10–11 Benedict Blaythwayt; 12–13 Georgie Birkett; 14–15 Annabel Spenceley; 14bl Andrea Norton; 15cr, br, bc Scot Ritchie; 17l Steve Lach; 17r Scot Ritchie; 18–21 Ellen Beier; 20–21 (globes) Julian Baker; 22–23 Annabel Spenceley; 23tr, cr, br Scot Ritchie; 24–25 Annabel Spenceley; 24t , 25tl, tr, cr, br Georgie Birkett; 26 c, bl, br Georgie Birkett; 27r Scot Ritchie.

Photographs

The publishers would like to thank the following for permission to reproduce photographs:
7t Sally & Richard Greenhill; 7b Latha Menon; 8–9 Life File; 16 Image Bank.